On Speaking Terms

Ruth J. Rapp
Minnesota
Writers
Collection

Books by Connie Wanek

On Speaking Terms
Hartley Field
Bonfire

CONNIE WANEK

On Speaking Terms

COPPER CANYON PRESS

PORT TOWNSEND, WASHINGTON

Cover art: Odilon Redon, *Pepper and Lemon on a White Tablecloth*, 1901. Oil on canvas, 46 x 28 cm. Collection of the Gemeentemuseum Den Haag.

Copper Canyon Press is in residence at Fort Worden State Park in Port Townsend, Washington, under the auspices of Centrum. Centrum is a gathering place for artists and creative thinkers from around the world, students of all ages and backgrounds, and audiences seeking extraordinary cultural enrichment.

Grateful acknowledgment is given to the following publications where many of these poems first appeared: *The Atlantic Monthly, The Bloomsbury Review, Flurry, Great River Review, Luna, Narrative, North Coast Review, Poetry, Poetry East, Speakeasy, Tarpaulin Sky, To Topio, Turtle, Water-Stone Review.* Several poems first appeared in *North Country Sampler,* a project to benefit artists in crisis, published by Calyx Press in 2005.

"A Random Gust from the North" won the 2003 Jane Kenyon Poetry Prize from *Water-Stone Review.*

"Pickles" appeared in a collaborative print/poetry project, *Shared Visions,* and its accompanying exhibition publication from Calyx Press, 2004.

The author would like to thank the Witter Bynner Foundation for Poetry, the Arrowhead Regional Arts Council, the Minnesota State Arts Board, and the Loft Literary Center for their generous support. She would also like to thank Ted Kooser for his immeasurable kindness.

LIBRARY OF CONGRESS CATALOGING-IN-PUBLICATION DATA
Wanek, Connie, 1952–
  On speaking terms / Connie Wanek.
    p. cm.
  ISBN 978-1-55659-294-2
  I. Title.
  PS3573.A4768O605 2010
  811'.54—dc22

                         2009029434

98765432 FIRST PRINTING

COPPER CANYON PRESS
Post Office Box 271
Port Townsend, Washington 98368
www.coppercanyonpress.org

for Phil, Hannah, and Casey

CONTENTS

ONE

TWO

THREE

On Speaking Terms

ONE

First Snow

There were snows before I can remember,
famous snows that buried sheep alive,
Florida snows settling like pollen into orange blossoms,
and the first snow, a blizzard
drifting against the locked gate of Eden.

Afterward it was Eve who made
the first snowman, her second sin, and she laughed
as she rolled up the wet white carpet
and lifted the wee head into place.
"And God causeth the sun to melt her labors,
for He was a jealous God."

This time of year we count our summer blessings:
a series of disasters that passed south of us.
We walk the trails we'll soon be skiing;
you take my hand and tuck the knot they make
into your coat pocket. Each breath
is a little cloud capable of a single snowflake.

Monopoly

We used to play, long before we bought real houses.
A roll of the dice could send a girl to jail.
The money was pink, blue, gold as well as green,
and we could own a whole railroad
or speculate in hotels where others dreaded staying:
the cost was extortionary.

At last one person would own everything,
every teaspoon in the dining car, every spike
driven into the planks by immigrants,
every crooked mayor.
But then, with only the clothes on our backs,
we ran outside, laughing.

Nothing

there are twelve hours in the day, and above fifty in the night

Marie de Rabutin-Chantal

Nothing knew the time as she did,
but that was all she knew.
She stood at the window and watched
as snowclouds stole past like heavy-laden thieves
through a sky where nothing could hide
or be hidden,
where light steps accumulated through the hours
to vanish later in the sun.
She looked in on the sleeping children
and found them grown,
their heads and feet leagues apart,
their comforters thrown off
in their wild thrashing rest.
For each light that died, two lit up,
yet darkness endured.
So much labor led nowhere. So many words
led only to silence.
Nothing could be done at such an hour
but even that was more than she could do.

Tracks in the Snow

How was it I did not see that lofty sky before?
And how happy I am to have found it at last.

Tolstoy's Prince Andrey

He lived in the house closest to the cemetery
and after a fresh snow
he liked to ski among the headstones.
New graves had an incline and a downward slope
that was gently exhilarating.
If people cared they never said so,
and his tracks were plainly legible,
a practiced signature
leading to and from his door.
He was as honest as the snow.

Old graves had settled and grown flatter
though he could still feel them under his skis.
Some years the snow rose so deep
that even the headstones were buried.
Then the quiet intensified, and he could forget
it was a graveyard
but for those rare occasions when, midstride,
he stabbed his pole into the snow
and struck granite.

Rarely, but sometimes,
he fell: a lapse in concentration,
and then he thought,
"That's all it takes," and lying there,
"This is how it will be."
His skis formed an X at his feet
and the heart he seldom consulted
made itself known to him,

throbbing urgently in his ears:

Get up, get up, get up, get up.

The Accordion

for Hannah

It was the one tangible you brought home
from the city, an armful of instrument,
bellows and keys and buttons and a smell
of antique lubrication, and a sound that poured
undiminished through solid walls.
You sat in your chair with its straps around your shoulders
teaching yourself to play,
determined to do different things differently
in the tradition of your people,
mixed-breeds from a dozen lands.
You sat as at a dance
with your partner on your lap, but it was also
a baby you were coaxing to speak.
I carried you that same way long ago,
your infant head under my chin, your chest against my chest,
my arms around you, my little marsupial.
I have photos of us like that. Mother and child.
And more. . . I can feel it physically. . . my arms still ache. . .
it's like phantom pain after an amputation,
phantoms being real.
                    You left it here with us,
the accordion, debating
whether to sell it, or to indulge yourself
by retaining such a large artifact, as it troubled no one
tucked back in your closet
in its battered, leather-covered case,
though neither was it useful.
Except it came to us at such a time:
you sat alone with it for hours
before your open curtains,
the music book awash in winter light,

hesitations, repetitions, small masteries,
and beyond you
snow passed through the sieve of the pine boughs
with the delicacy of grace notes.

Scrabble

I hoped to find solace in my letters,
perhaps even love,
a lover, or simply lovely.
I'm too old, too nervous for this endeavor.

Where are the words when it's my turn
to ask an honest question of the president?
My adversaries stare. . .
If only I could compose myself!

I need a *t* to give me time—
a *p* and I'd have help.
It's the story of my life,
rearranging assets and coming up shor.

At last I settle on an *s* that I can add
to something someone else has said,
making, of just one,
an infinite number of mistakes.

Directions

First you'll come to the end of the freeway.
Then it's not so much north on Woodland Avenue
as it is a feeling that the pines are taller and weigh more,
and the road, you'll notice,
is older with faded lines and unmown shoulders.
You'll see a cemetery on your right
and another later on your left.
Sobered, drive on.

                    Drive on for miles
if the fields are full of hawkweed and daisies.
Sometimes a spotted horse
will gallop along the fence. Sometimes you'll see
a hawk circling, sometimes a vulture.
You'll cross the river many times
over smaller and smaller bridges.
You'll know when you're close;
people always say they have a sudden sensation
that the horizon, which was always far ahead,
is now directly behind them.
At this point you may want to park
and proceed on foot, or even
on your knees.

Drunkard's Path

It wasn't love, she said.
But they were married
in their seventies, his first,
her second. Every calendar
she marked the anniversary
of the day her true love died.
She made soap in the basement,
better than you could buy,
out of cheap fat and lye.
The silence was deep and comforting.
Words limited experience
to what they meant,
when what she felt was
like the sea, always moving,
and always heavy.
Looking back it seemed their lives
were like a drunkard's path,
pieced together from the good parts
of worn-out clothes,
and so many accidents were involved,
so much sewing under a bad light,
so many needlepricks.
And what's this,
he asked, lifting a raw edge.
It's called drunkard's path—
and his shoulders stiffened.
Turn each block ninety degrees
and the whole quilt looks
orderly instead. It's that easy,
like moving the two hands of the clock
with one finger.

White Roads

We hitched the black pony to the cutter
and set out on the white road.
I liked to be the one to hold the reins,
to stand and shake the long reins
and feel the sudden lurch
of a promising beginning.

The country was quiet before snowmobiles.
A neighbor's dog barked at ours
as she raced beside us, and the wind
hooted across our red ears. Too,
there were crows, there were always crows,
cawing so hard they seemed to be vomiting.

I only knew the road as far as Doc's woods
one way, and the school the other.
Town was as remote as Rome.
We passed the shack owned by mean brothers.
We passed the frozen pond where summer's cows
had waded, muddy and content.

I seldom left my world then,
and little entered it. Too much was close at hand
to wonder what became of the sun all night,
the stars all day.
Or where the snow went that lay
so deep upon the roads.

Lipstick

She leaned over the sink,
her weight on her toes,
and applied lipstick
in quick certain strokes
the way a man signs
his hundredth autograph
of the morning.
She tested a convictionless smile
as the lipstick retracted
like a red eel.
All day she left her mark
on everything she kissed,
even the air,
like intoxicating news
whispered from ear to ear:
He left it all to me.

Jacks

Up goes the ball every morning.
So much to do while it's in the air!
Then at noon, the thundering bounce
and an afternoon spent
in delicate panic
before the palm opens, quite full,
to admit the ball anyway.
Now sleep if you can.
Tomorrow will prove
a trifle harder.

Everything Free

The lake and sky were quarreling along the horizon:
late September. Whose fault was that?
The birches unburdened themselves
of the thinnest leaves in memory.

Where an old man had lived alone in quiet squalor
the yard was filled with boxes
and a sign: EVERYTHING FREE.
He'd finally done as he'd promised;

he'd gone to Arizona to pan for gold.
People milled about, curious and disgusted,
and when every box had been overturned,
the shredded, chipped, tarnished, water-soaked and smelly

goods determined to be irredeemable,
someone finally called the police.
The supply of clouds was inexhaustible, and the lake
had the sheen of titanium:

these were our riches.
There were gentler places to be poor.
People said he lived as he did because he was lazy
or lonely, but I believe

we all end up with what we really want.
Look around. You wanted this.
And I wanted one thing to remember him by
and took the sign.

Fishing on Isabella Lake

The lake was big enough to have islands,
a sign of wealth. . . my islands. . .
We saw a campsite on the largest
as we paddled by. No one there yet.
It was no particular day.
It was just day.

Once you could get far enough away,
but now you carry money with you even here.
The portage smelled like dust
and fish guts—a little altar on a stone,
a pile of viscera and heads, shining with prompt flies:
someone cleaned a few small walleyes.
Don't be sorry—they felt nothing.

Nothing you would recognize anyway,
though you've jabbed your thumb on lures,
and you've swum naked in a lake
without your glasses,
and your breathing has been labored,
your eyes stung by the sun.
At your most vulnerable moment
something rose in the periphery,
dangerous and indistinct, a rough underwater boulder
big enough to dump a canoe into the whitecaps
before you could even think a warning.

Save what you can, quickly—
but that gets harder and harder.
The lakes are low, drought and record heat,
southern summers creeping north
trailing their poisonous snakes
into Minnesota, a no-fault state
where we blame everyone, or no one.

I lost a fish at the canoe
without even seeing it.
My lure, suddenly free, leapt back at me.
I knew the fish was big
by the quality of its panic,
the line it drew against the drag.
I hated to lose it—I swore like a man.
One moment I looked into the lake
and it seemed full; the next moment, empty.

We smelled bear on the portage
but saw only an early star
burning through the jack pines—*ursa absentia.*
Not a star, but a planet with an accusatory stare.
We had the sun in common and little else.
Ours was the Goldilocks orbit,
not too hot, not too cold.
A day on the water
and all we could think of was sleep,
sleep and the lost fish.
We take things; we leave things behind—
and the sum of all this is zero,
or rather, one more day.

Garlic

A head of garlic swells
like a hobo's bundle. Pried open,
it's equally pungent.
Fresh garlic is good for you
if you crave solitude
and the open road.
Once I wrote a word
on the delicate paper I tore
from a garlic clove, a whimsy
that came out of my pores.
The word is gone, not forgotten,
like the man I lived with then.
Sometimes moderation is
not an option.
He's always in your bed;
he's never in your bed.
Garlic is or isn't in a dish
or sprouting
on the sunny windowsill,
an inch of green ambition
and a stirring
in the severed roots.

Bald Eagle

Your image is on my credit card,
you and the old red, white, and blue.
Each purchase receives your scrutiny
if not approbation: yes,
I should buy less chocolate and more fish.
You're on my green bills, too,
an endorsement of bold shopping habits,
of soaring to Target and descending,
talons outstretched.
I saw you once beside the freeway
perched in a naked winter tree
waiting for fatalities, presumably.
You have to be practical; meat is meat.
Even the emblem
of the United States of America
must eat.

Rags

I dust with a sleeve I loved
to look at on my arm.
Blue is gray now, like a patch
of sky filthy with clouds.
Why is piano dust always so gray?
Something about sound waves
and decay
that science could explain.

I didn't need scissors
the cotton was so rotted
by sun and sweat, the salt I made,
the sticky seawater. I was glad
to actually wear something out,
to have seen one thing
completely through,
even though I'd miss
being the person who wore it.

Hoarfrost

Hoarfrost coated the lawn
like a fine white mold.
I stood in the doorway
at the border
as cold crossed the threshold.
The air was medicine,
a vaccine: a small dose of illness
so the body would rally
against the pestilence to come.
I closed my eyes—
a small dose of darkness.
The sun was furious as it rose,
but it always seemed angry,
even at midday
when it was most successful.

I had my work
in the blackened garden,
another summer to cut loose
and carry in my arms
to the repository of summers,
the heap of refuse
beyond the raspberry canes.
But I left the chrysanthemums
to freeze and live,
to feed the passing monarchs
from the pungency
of their defiance.

Lady

When I was young and lived on a farm
all our dogs were called "Lady"
even if they proved to be gentlemen.
We took in strays,
drop-offs that trotted across our fields
after town cars sped away.
Perhaps a child had turned to stare
through the back window. Freedom.
Like the end of a second marriage.
At least the dogs had a chance in the country;
it wasn't the pound.
The last Lady before we left the farm
was too shy to eat
while anyone watched.
She had low self-esteem perhaps,
but enormous litters, eight and nine and ten
not counting the doomed runts.
The neighbor's roaming collie
was the father; once I saw him (as I thought)
hurting her and I struck him with a shovel.
Well. He ran off the moment he could, of course.
Freedom. She looked up at me
with simple, fathomless eyes
and licked my dirty hand.
It wasn't thanks; it was acquiescence.
I think she was a Buddhist;
she bent in every wind, while her roots
went deeper and deeper.
When we left the farm we had to give her
to neighbors, the Tremls,
Joe, Jim, Judy, John, and Jenny.

Confessional Poem

I never told him anything
he didn't expect—
the white lies of a small girl,
a week's accumulations
related in halting, mouselike whispers.
He blessed me anyway
and gave me my penance
and bade me go in peace.
Perhaps the next penitent
would offer him what he came for,
a great, meaty, mortal sin like adultery
described in gorgeous language,
words that lit up the confessional
like a flashlight in a closet:
a silk cuff missing its button,
sheer stockings coiled on the floor,
shoes with heels like wineglass stems—
the hypnotic black-and-white images of film noir,
wherein all eyes followed a bad star
with uncontrollable longing.

God Rest Ye Merry Gentlemen

Up and down the bar
a dozen conversations turned to arguments,
and Christ was oft mentioned.
None drank his blood
but ordered stronger spirits, clear or pale gold.
People grew bored waiting for Moses, too—
some never liked him anyway,
another Mr. Know-It-All,
and why so self-assured after forty years
of wrong turns? And what made so many women
look at him that way?

Who needs manna in a bar?
Let hot be hot and cold be cold,
let the stone be hard and heavy.
If we must stagger, let us stagger,
and if we last till morning,
forgive us.

TWO

Walking Distance

for Stanley Dentinger (1922–2004)

Walking distance used to be much farther,
miles and miles.

Your grandfather, as a young man
with a wife and new baby son,

walked to and from
his job, which was in the next town.

That was Iowa, 1946,
and it was not a hardship

but "an opportunity," which is youth speaking,
and also a particular man

of German descent, walking on good legs
on white gravel roads,

smoking cigarettes which were cheap
though not free as they'd been

during the war. Tobacco
burned toward his fingers, but never

reached them. The fire was small and personal,
almost intimate, glowing bright

when he put the cigarette to his lips
and breathed through it.

So many cigarettes before bombing runs
and none had been his last,

a great surprise. Sometimes he passed
a farmer burning field grass in the spring,

the smoldering line advancing toward the fence.
He had to know what he was doing,

so near the barn. You had to be close
to see the way

blades of dry grass passed the flame along
at a truly individual level,

very close to see how delicious a meal
the field was to the fire

on a damp, calm, almost English morning
ideal for walking.

Popcorn

Or else while sleeping I had drifted back to an earlier stage in my life,
now for ever outgrown

Proust

I woke in the night to the smell of popcorn
on a Sunday afternoon,
quarts and quarts eaten one kernel at a time.
The football game was on:
Lions and Packers, Bears and Packers,
Vikings and Packers.
My father still wore his tennis shorts
after five sets of doubles that morning
at the college courts: our ritual,
our Sunday assemblage
with a congregation of the eternally devoted,
all dressed in white like a choir
singing out love, love, love,
which in tennis means not charity
but humility. The cold desert night
loitered in the shade, while
our beloved sun blessed image after image:
new balls, woolly as sheep,
white as the Host served to each in turn,
our rackets molded of steamed wood,
strung with gut,
leather grips black with old sweat,
an upturned face seeking the rapture of an ace.
My shadow swung its shadow racket,
striking the shadow ball that flew forth to land
directly under the genuine ball,
a conjunction perfectly timed, like an eclipse.
We knew the dimensions of the court

so well that we felt each white line
as one feels an acupuncture pin
tugging on remote, related nerves.
My father liked to win but didn't mind losing,
while I hated to lose but didn't like winning.
I loved to run every ball down
like a young dog fetching endlessly on the lawn.
By noon our blood
was surging in and out of our hearts
and our lungs were full as sails.
The balls were light now, sheared by blow after blow.
Someday I would hit the last tennis ball of my life—
just long, or more likely, into the net.
At last we shook hands, friend and foe,
and drove home, a fine white salt on our bodies
and embedded in our clothes
as though we'd bathed in the Dead Sea.
Then I poured corn into the hot pan;
a half cup could expand
to feed multitudes, to fill a bowl
the size of a sink. Here was our indulgence,
the reward we gave ourselves
for doing, once again, exactly as we liked.

The Splits

The world of my youth was divided
into girls who could and girls who couldn't
slide casually to the floor,
one leg aft and one fore, while their faces
retained a sprightly cheer.
All summer, all year
they stretched the critical tendons,
descending in increments
the way the willful enter a frigid lake,
their arms folded across their chests,
their backs burning in the sun
as their legs numb.
Yet the splits seemed less a skill
than a gift of birth: Churchillian pluck
combined with a stroke of luck
like a pretty face with a strong chin.
One felt that even as babies
some girls were predispositioned.

Buttercups

Corot's floating blooms (the tip of his brush
touches the canvas) a drop of cream
suspended over deep woodland green,
(the scent of sun-warmed oils)
daisies, too, and something blue and tall, a harebell
(the palette crowded like a plaza)
with stems like wires that carry light
(the white sap that beads
when the weed is cut) up from the earth,

(how anything wild can remain so clean)
an afternoon that is the lifetime of a blossom
(a bee asking to be painted, a commission!)
the buttercup shining as though varnished
(clouds slowing as the wind falls)
or waxed, even in the shade
(as though each sensation could be expressed
as a distinct tint) even in the lapel of a cotton smock.

Closest to the Sky

for Casey

I still feel like I'm trespassing
when I climb the attic stairs to your old room,
in all the house the place closest to the sky.
Signs of your former occupation:
mostly software—inessential shirts and socks—
and silver discs with whole worlds
collapsed into them,
worlds you conquered and tired of.
You left a tin of pennies on your dresser;
a guitar pick on the floor,
a blue triangle with softened points
and, if I had the dust and brushes,
your fingerprints.

These days your bed is never disturbed.
Here you lay for many weeks
healing after the accident. Perhaps that's why
both you and I avoid this place now.
Out the window an ancient spruce so near,
little more than arm's length: I can see every needle,
dull in the winter, sober green-gray,
a peaceful color
that never tries to cheer us falsely.
You used to complain about the crows
that woke you at daybreak
when they landed on the roof, a whole flock
shuffling overhead, cawing hard, calling for you.
Often I heard you swear at them out the window.
Now you're gone, but the crows only know
that no one here is angry anymore.

Comb

This comb has been here since my son left home.
When I run my thumb across its teeth
it makes a rough hum.
Stamped in gold are these words:
GENUINE ACE HARD RUBBER.
That's not much to go on, and really,
I don't care whence it came,
what wind blew it in. What concerns me
is how long I should keep it,
whether he might ever need it, miss it,
whether he has any memory of its parting
his hair on one side, then the other,
as he stood exactly here
before the mirror in the morning light
untangling the night.

The Buck

He looked done in
as he grazed, pawed, and grazed again
at the frozen compost pile.
He'd appeared in our yard in town
on the first day of hunting season, as if he knew
the closer you get to what you fear
the safer you are.
Could he see us at the window?
He startled once and stared up at the house,
his antlers wide open—
I had never seen such a rack of spikes.
Yet the roots deep in his skull
were rotten now; soon his antlers
would drop off into the snow.
Had he been a good king?
I doubt it. But another
would have done as he had, given the chance,
and most of his conquests were achieved
through intimidation alone.
He was gray as bark as he limped back
into the twilight of the woods,
hard as a fact that is
in the middle of changing.

O Little Town

a hymn for Morgan Park, Minnesota

The king is in his grave, the woods are cut,
the water is sour, the steel plant
whose towers held unrepentant infidels,
whose fires melted stone, is gone.

Some earth never froze, those days,
and nights were red below smoke and steam.
An empty house filled again, and the church
pews were packed, a man of the cloth

leaning over the pulpit, raising
his pointing finger, shouting himself hoarse.
People called any old thing a miracle
and the rest was the Lord's wrath.

In the aftermath, when the plant
stopped growing and then began to die,
slain by foreigners, the little town
wrote its last will and testament,

which was a song.
How still we see thee lie, dark streets,
tributaries of the passing river
that men drive across in December.

Sometimes they fall through the ice
and sometimes they don't,
roaring up the far bank, tires spinning,
sick to death of the old women.

Umbrella

When I push your button
you fly off the handle,
old skin and bones,
black bat wing.

We're alike, you and I.
Both of us
resemble my mother,
so fierce in her advocacy

on behalf of
the most vulnerable child
who'll catch his death
in this tempest.

Such a headwind!
Sometimes it requires
all my strength
just to end a line.

But when the wind is at
my back, we're likely
to get carried away, and say
something we can never retract,

something saturated from the ribs
down, an old stony
word like *ruin.* You're what roof
I have, frail thing,

you're my argument
against the whole sky.
You're the fundamental difference
between wet and dry.

Placebo

At last she could sigh without coughing,
her rib cage quiet,
her heart at rest on its perch.

She regarded the world calmly
without the filter
of her suffering, long fouled

by seasons of maladies and melancholia.
Truly, she had faith
each time she felt the pill on her tongue

and swallowed it whole with a sip of wine,
a tablespoon of intoxication
integral to the cure. All she asked

was to feel as others felt,
those who didn't need
to interrogate each sensation,

who didn't find the same troubled face
in every mirror
that was like the false sky

filling the east window. A sudden thump meant
another warbler.
It was never the glass that broke.

Picture Yourself

. . .off the Gunflint Trail

A few ripples on the lake
folding themselves over like anonymous notes.
An idle day. Time slows here, as they say
it does in space; the minutes elongated,
lying in a long row in the sun,
stretching out, softening.
You ate your sandwich on the rocks
while your canoe waited like a dog on a leash:
it has all the fidelity (you were thinking),
all the eagerness of a spaniel.
It was company.

After dozens of failures
you finally remembered the camera.
You mounted it on a tripod of boulders
and composed the scene around
a missing man: you'd have ten seconds
to scramble into place
and turn back
before the shutter took its tiny bite.
This was exposure number twenty-three
on the mystery roll installed seasons ago
at Christmas (always, if nothing else, Christmas).
The camera saw what you saw
but it remembered.

Yet it felt nothing.
Only you knew the truth: not what you've done
but what you've felt
and wanted. Not what you've saved, either,
through years of supposed self-denial,

but all you've spent, and where,
such as there, a day alone on the water
revising your epitaph.

Was it vanity to arrange
the wilderness as your backdrop,
to motion the tamarack
a little to the left?
The woods answer only to the sun and wind.
Cedars lined the far shore with their roots
well below the waterline, cedars with their burden
of near invincibility.

The color wouldn't be right. It never is.
One day you'd hold the photo and try to explain
how green it was that day,
how the quiet seemed to build to a crescendo,
the inertia to a climax.
How you wondered at your heart
beating past such a moment.

You adjusted the camera, worried about the battery:
old and bad, no doubt.
Perhaps it wouldn't matter
because the available light. . .
and here you paused, looking up. . .
Not a cloud. How often does this happen?

The Death of My Father

He died at different times in different places.
In Wales he died tomorrow,
which doesn't mean his death was preventable.
It had been coming for years,
crossing the ocean, the desert, pausing often,
moving like water or wind,
here turned aside by a stone,
then hurried where the way was clear.

Once I lay on my back in the grass and watched
as cloud after cloud moved east
and disintegrated. The mystery now
is not where they went but how
I could ever have been so idle.

Funerals are all the same.
I saw him cry at his mother's wake
when I was young enough to be
picked up, lofted into someone's arms.
He, a man, cried that day,
but people smiled, too. You think now
you want to be remembered,
but the dead don't care.
My grandmother's face said that.

Indifference is a great relief, after a lifetime
of mothering one's many worries,
trying not to play favorites.

I wasn't present when he died.
I feel that keenly, that I should have
had a share. I was spared
unfairly. I was not fed
the bitter broth and the hard bread.

What time did it happen
exactly? What was I doing at that exact moment?
What can I do now?

But the moment is never exact.
One dies over years—yes, there is a first breath
and a last, yet consider a cut tulip
upright in a vase, closing as the day ends,
then turning toward the morning window, opening again.
One day I touch a petal and it falls off.
Even so the balding stem takes
another sip of water.

My mother held the phone to his ear
so each middle-aged child could say a distant goodbye,
and she searched his face for a sign.
Perhaps. No one knows what he heard
or if a phone was essential to it.
The longing to believe is more enduring
than any truth—truth is so perishable.
I once was found, but now I'm lost.
I could see, but now I'm blind.

Walking to Work

Had thunder come from the sun?
No, a single cloud crossed
the great, dry autumn sky,
a cloud whose cells divided as I watched.

All around me leaves,
light as tracing paper,
fell at the rain's first touch.

Then a loose hound spotted me,
and I braced myself.
Evasion was simply not possible;
I would have to play.

I would smell of wet dog all day,
and faintly of rain.
Now the cloud drifted over the lake

while the streets were steaming.
In nine long hours I'd be walking home again
to white chrysanthemums
that had opened in my absence,

blooming in the shadow of the house
like candles lit
in an iron lantern.

A Sighting

The gray owl had seen us and had fled
but not far. We followed noiselessly,
driving him from pine to pine:
I will not let thee go except thou bless me.

He flew as though it gave him no pleasure,
forcing himself from the bough,
falling until his wings caught him:
they had to stroke hard, like heavy oars.

He must have just eaten
something that had, itself, just eaten.
Finally he crossed the swamp and vanished
as into a new day, hours before us,

and we stood near the chest-high reeds,
our feet sinking, and felt
we'd been dropped suddenly from midair
back into our lives.

Skiing at Gooseberry Falls

The dangerous water was approachable,
the falls paralyzed—
like a tranquilized polar bear.
The ice had yellowed, but the snow was fresh—
no one had taken possession of it
until we dropped our skis.

You broke trail and I followed,
shuffling, knee-deep.
The river took us back and up
to flatter country, while behind us
two blue lines unscrolled
and the punctures of our poles
were evidence of chronic instability.
Other impressions testified
to the times I'd fallen—it happens so quickly
when one's thoughts stray.
How fondly I had planned this day
and now my eyes were tearing in the wind,
proving that we cry for many reasons.
Your beard was shaggy with ice
when you turned back to me:
Have you had enough?

We were miles from the car. The cold
was massive, like an invisible mountain.
Far off, on Lake Superior, steam rose
over a patch of open water
as though anything above freezing was boiling.
Of course not. And you laughed
and pushed on,
bound to your slippery shadow.

Green Tent

Erect, the green tent is a gable,
the attic of the earth.
We enter on hands and knees,
by means of a long zipper
delicately undone.
Inside we're still outside,
still vulnerable
to a leaning pine or a bear
rummaging through the pantry.
The walls are green drapes;
they're a green balloon
we filled by sighing.
It's home, though, a studio apartment
you invited me to
where the only place to sit
is the bed.

Pumpkin

None is so poor that he need sit on a pumpkin.

Thoreau

To write as a field grows pumpkins,
to scribble page after page with an orange crayon,
to lose teeth and still smile,
to survive a frost that blackened acres,
to wake after surgery.

To live without rotting from within,
to ignore imperfections of the skin,
to be heavy, and still be chosen,
to please a strict vegetarian,
to end the day full of light.

THREE

A Random Gust from the North

Runoff

Another hottest summer ever.
Storms with the violence of a broken atom.
Storms that drove the boats in
and smashed them in their slips. Power out for days,
so we lived by the sky, like any animal.
Runoff turned the bay red
as from some ancient slaughter—
the smelt runs, perhaps, every spring of your youth
when fish crowded the river mouths
so thickly you could reach down with only your hands
and take all you wanted
and people did. In the evening
we knelt on the boulders by the big lake
and washed our forearms
in the surges that rose against the stone,
and the water we loved was cold enough to kill us.

Sunfish

His ribs were thick as barrel staves,
his heart full of chambers such as waves
carve out of granite,
smooth caverns accessible only by boat.
His toes were like mushrooms,
misshapen by the sealed can of a boot.
They had the look of fish bait
as indeed they were
when as a child he sat on the weathered dock,
the soft gray boards, his feet
dangling in the lake, and sunfish
nibbled his toes. Sunnies.
What was death, but sunlight on the water?

Now he set herring nets on summer mornings
while the village slept. His boat was unnamed,
a workboat among the pleasure craft
in the marina. Nothing polished,
no illusions, no vanity.
He left the harbor on an open palm
held out to the lake and sky.
He was an offering.
Good days he filled the boat with thrashing fish
drowning in oxygen. It was the same fish
over and over, like page after page
to the illiterate.
This man with a kind disposition
sold his catch, and thus he lived.
"North," he said, and the word itself
spoke, offering hardship and darkness and solitude,
and he trembled like a compass needle.

South Wind

Sometimes he caught a fish that had cancer.
A south wind carried the stench of the paper mill.
South. A single city sixty miles across.
Thousands of cars on the freeway,
all sizes and sorts, like fish
forced together by low water
or by a net. The air he was obliged to breathe,
air that had passed through
smokestacks and motors and ducts and countless
living lungs before his and after,
air that had a history,
that had come to the city years ago
blown in from the alfalfa fields
to enter a copse of mirrored towers
now seen, now lost in the sky,
to swirl in a courtyard

rising and falling through the hours
without passion or purpose
but with exhilarating ease.
Flocks of ravens gathered in the dirty park,
shining like the jewelry of the Aztecs
polished by slaves.
Heat waves rose from the grid, a conflagration
that seared the silver bellies of the jets.
There were highways among the clouds
or else the sky was but another blue sea
and planes were passenger ships,
as birds were fish,
as wind was a current.
Why lament? So goes the wind. South.
Here is the puncture
where poison entered the body.

    A Small Vessel in the Swells

He took up the rope
and drew the boat toward him like a pony.
It woke as he stepped into it
and settled obediently under his weight.
Then the canter of a small vessel in the swells,
the bow high, power
from the churning hindquarters.
He went out against the will of the lake.
The water red as the sunrise:
he was crossing the sky.
Later it would be rough,
perhaps dangerous,
the warning repeated every few seconds
until it goes unheeded.
Where does a wave begin?
Before memory,
in the quick pulse of a mother's blood

pouring into the bay of the womb.
Impossible to say whether the water
speaks from within or without.
Ashore again, he felt the earth
rock on its fulcrum; standing on shore
he felt land-sick, drained, short of breath.

The North Shore

A cabin so small it is like a woodpecker hole
smelling of fresh pine pitch.
Like a new-made pauper's coffin.
Calm today. One feels the depth of the lake,
the weight of an iron anchor
falling through the fathoms.
Here or there a surface disturbance,
a boat wake, a few gulls bickering over fish offal,
then a random gust from the north.
The lake wrinkles the way a horse,
dozing in the shade, jerks its skin
where a fly lands.
Waves come to shore backward, blindly,
like a horse backing into wagon traces
with a sack over its head.
If a horse knew its strength
it could never be tamed.

A Last Reading

The north pole. Instruments alone confirm it.
And what if the instruments disagree?
Can there be such an absolute arrival?
Or does realization come later,
far too late for the champagne?
And what of ambition?
Surely it precedes a man by months, years,

and has already published its memoirs.
Here one senses the attention
of every compass in the world
pointing like a crowd of fingers
toward a tightrope stretched between
clouds. A lone figure looks everywhere
but down. So much light,
light to spare, light to spread on the ice like salt.
The pole afloat; we are neither first
nor last, though perhaps nearer the last.
We need no instruments.
The equatorial vertigo subsides;
the heat of exertion dissipates.
We have no fear of falling.
We can never be lost.

Musical Chairs

The music, quavering and faint,
had somehow kept order among us.
But when it stopped
everyone rushed toward the lifeboats
where seats were scandalously insufficient.

Why had our parents given birth to so many of us?
They expected us to share, perhaps,
or they couldn't imagine science failing in the end,
unsinkable science, the laboratory of miracles
where mice lived as quietly as they could.

Perhaps the sea would take us all finally,
perhaps the earth. Meanwhile
a tranquilizing waltz began
and we left the safety of our seats. The line of us,
which was really a circle, began to inch forward.

A Parting

after Wang Wei

Mother:

We have to say goodbye again so soon.
Another seam torn open, another hole in the pocket
discovered too late.
You're going where the snow falls
as rain; you're leaving
through the gate that opened in a wall of clouds:
go quickly.
Call me every night unless you're happy.
Then I can tell myself
that all the silent evenings
are what I want.

Son:

You've done all you can—be satisfied.
More and my thanks would be
like tea steeped too long,
tinged with bitterness.
The bear is dreaming somewhere under the snow
but I can't sleep for thinking of the road
that changes color: gray here, yellow in the south.
Don't worry. I'll greet the wild goose for you,
the one you fed all summer
in the reeds by the wide river.

Dog Days

Call it selfishness. Call it self-preservation.
We need ignorance,
a day on the water without the chatter
that pours out of the television,
without the picture that requires a thousand words
to disarm. We need the pines
that have stood through two hundred winters,
and the insects that live only a few hours.

Surely the planet will mend behind us
as water heals behind the canoe.
Cruelties in the fossil record are cruelties no more.
It seems our wrongs spring from our right
to pursue our own happiness,
which is a red fox running before the dogs,
dying in their teeth.

It's still too cold for clouds of blackflies.
Some creatures require a blood meal,
but why blood? Why not honey?
Why not plain clear water blessed by the sun?
A moose learns to be a moose—what else should it be?
We're always trying to be gods, I think,
without agreement on what is holy.
Our doctrine requires us to wander all day
in the wilderness, meeting no one
and grateful for that, though out here
they'd likely be our kind and take our side:
the paddle-bearers, the water-people.

Monkey See

What he saw, he did, if he could.
A stick was a gun, a rock a bomb.
He threw it up and it came down
and landed in the sandbox
smashing a solid little house
that he could reerect by pressing
mud into a plastic cup
and dumping it over.
Play was work, his craft,
his long informal apprenticeship
into the ancient guild
of vandals.

Pecans

The travelers brought us pecans from Las Cruces
and I saw again the place I lived so long,
where the Rio Grande flows wide and shallow.
I saw my father with his eyes closed,
basking in the early sun,
sipping a cup of strong black coffee.
I saw my mother pacing the dry yard, planning
the pear and apple trees she'd grown up north
that suffered so during desert summers.
I stood again at the kitchen sink, looking out,
my hands idle in the dishwater,
and watched a vagrant stoop in the back alley
to fill his pockets with fallen pecans.
He was passing through, heading for the coast,
guided by instinct like waterfowl.
Why we must go we can't say.
Some blame the heavens, the restless stars,
some the earth, spinning under our feet
like a ball under an acrobat.

In the palm pecans resemble a clutch of wild eggs,
brown and oblong, full of blueprints.
The trees themselves were the pride of the yard;
their green shelter and the scent of their shade
reminded Mother of her Wisconsin.
When we walked beneath them in late fall
we stepped on pecans, and they cracked
against the dry earth. Sometimes we all pitched in
to pick them up, all the sisters and brothers,
working under threat of punishment, or cajoled with bribes.
In those days we owned a black border collie
that ran away every night
with every intention of coming home,

though one night she finally didn't.
I wonder at those
who stay in the same place their whole lives;
I wonder where I'll die.
At some point we just want what's easiest.

Pecans are not native to Las Cruces;
they need far more rain than falls in the desert.
But water flows all summer from the river,
diverted through long muddy ditches,
and the trough of the valley
fills with greenery and bees. A place is both itself
and what we make of it, as we are ourselves
and what a place makes of us.
No Waneks at all are left in that town.

The travelers brought pecans, coarse and rustic,
the husk still attached to one or two,
here a bark fragment, a blade of blond grass.
I was glad to see them.
Only one pecan in perhaps a million sends out roots,
a sturdy green shoot,
and by some accidental or deliberate circumstance
becomes a tree that blooms and bears
year after year in the same soil.
The rest of the pecans are organized and eaten.
If this is sad, tell me what is not sad.

Portrait of a Gentleman

Then a cloud passed, and the pool was empty.

T.S. Eliot

1

He saw me strip a lilac from his hedge
and smiled as he supposed it afforded him
the slightest edge in what might come.
The blooms had not quite opened to the end
even while the first
had thinned and dried, like violet eyelids.
He called his dog and walked me to the bridge
("She's a champion bitch; her pups sell for a ransom")
and I told him she was handsome,
and she was, sleek and black with bold eyes
and a silver collar engraved with her name and his.

We stood and watched the water pass below,
passing and passing, yet always present,
shining even underneath our shadows,
and he spoke about a trout he'd caught downstream:
"Nothing to it really, but she was a fighter,
a brookie fat with eggs,
and I'd have let her go once I had her
but she took the hook too deep."
A hook, and the desperate fight against it.
I dropped the lilacs into the water and we watched them
turn and turn, trapped in an eddy.

2

I met him in the woods on tame city trails
where he broke the rules: his dog ran loose—
long strides, tail erect. Her leash tapped against

his pant leg as he stopped to say
he'd missed seeing me about. Had I gone away?
The leash was black to match the dog; she bounded
back to us as though jealous, her ears stiff,
her body flowing like smoke in the mild fall air.
She sniffed my outstretched hand once
and dismissed me.
"I come and go," I said, and he approved,
and held my elbow to guide me on the trail
as if I were in training.

Once we met when it was raining,
and spoke as one does in the half-dark
of second thoughts and misgivings.
He smelled of wet wool and tobacco, and his teeth
were gray (I saw gold when he smiled) and stained.
One felt winter bearing down,
nights falling slowly all afternoon, moon after moon
drawn through shredded clouds, a halo around
the noon sun spreading its ineffectual gospel
in the streets, the evergreens browning as though burned.
"If there's one thing I've learned," he said, "it's that
blood is blood. Her line is impeccable."

3

At last the kindest April came, and under the bridge
the water galloped, brown and white, like a steeplechase.
I saw his dog first, along the bank,
then he was at my elbow. "I ought to thank you,"
he said, "for your little note." I felt the reproach
though perhaps none was intended. He was confidential:
"When February ended, I passed the age my father was
when he died." Winter had spun like a coin in the air
to land safely in his open palm.
His dog was calm and heavy-bellied. "Yes, I had her bred.
This litter is the last."

We lost touch in the summer. I heard he'd gone
north to the lake after the pups were born.
I should have liked to see them, black and quick,
smooth as water flowing on either side of a life
and through it, too, nothing held back in their affections.
I wondered if he would keep them in spite of himself.
I wondered if I'd have taken one if he'd offered.
The thought tempted me since it was impossible—
if I'd held one in my arms, and felt its weight, its heat,
then no. . . thanks, but no. I'd have no trouble.

Immeasurable evenings, and soft violet skies;
night no more than a shadow cast for a few hours.
He was a man who liked his way, who knew his powers.
I walked freely in the woods, and past his house
where lights came on and burned in empty rooms
and sensors were positioned like baited mousetraps.
I walked all summer, especially when it rained,
and greens intensified and grew undisciplined
and the creek swelled with all the sky had lost
and the pools deepened, rich with trout.

Christmas Eve

I counted presents as I wrapped them,
making sure neither child was favored.
That year I had also given them the freedom
they'd long ago taken.

Watch, book, socks, money.
I could do this with my eyes closed.
This was the solitude I once craved,
this lonely task at the top of the house

in the old third-floor maid's room.
The silence was so complete that I heard
my scissors sever the very cells of the paper,
cutting a tree in half, decapitating Santa,

slicing the leather harness
so the reindeer leapt free of the sled.
I worked carefully, though in a few hours
all would be undone.

I stood up and stretched and went to the window,
the view I loved: birches in the snow,
the lake beyond, deep blue
and warmer than the day, a pine so close

I could leap out into its arms,
an old white pine hung with empty seed cones,
topped with a single preening crow
that shone like a black star.

Old Snow

Thaws have taken their toll,
and once rain fell across the white hills.
The snow is half ice now,
granulated and industrial, and the men
in the yard have lost their coal teeth
and are hollow-eyed and helpless.
They've been loyal to the picket line
all winter, watching scabs come and go.

Old snow has layers like a canyon wall,
a season precisely recorded,
what died when: fossilized crab apples
shaken loose by a historic wind,
feathers from a lost wren.
Soon the hardest snow will form
a black mirror on the road, and the luck
of this tough old town will turn.

Pickles

I don't need to say what they look like, do I?
Surely everyone who's bitten the end
off a stiff little gherkin
has had the same unwholesome thought.

The jars are nearly always short and stout
though pickles are not caloric.
With their broken dill and sunken detritus
the jars remind me of long-neglected aquariums;

and in fact we have some very old pickles
inhabiting a swampy corner of the fridge, passed over
time and again by a doubtful hand.

The pickles may be growing legs by now
and croaking all night
in the cold spring of the icebox, silenced
by the slightest movement of the door.

Coloring Book

Each picture is heartbreakingly banal,
a kitten and a ball of yarn,
a dog and bone.
The paper is cheap, easily torn.
A coloring book's authority is derived
from its heavy black lines
as unalterable as the Ten Commandments
within which minor decisions are possible:
the dog black and white,
the kitten gray.
Under the picture we find a few words,
a caption, perhaps a narrative,
a psalm or sermon.
But nowhere do we discover
a blank page where we might justify
the careless way we scribbled
when we were tired and sad
and could bear no more.

Blue Ink

Blue ink is friendlier than black,
more feminine. You can sign the papers
and still believe
it's not quite final.

You can conjecture in blue ink,
and write a check for more than you have.
People will understand.

Some days the lake is blue enough
to be bottled, or injected
directly into a pen,

though as the words dry
they disappear, letter by letter,
sparing you
serious embarrassment.

Jelly Beans

Three jelly beans remain in the bowl:
white, yellow, orange.
Glazed like tile, they shine in the lamplight,
the white one slightly apart,
bland and apologetic.
A full bowl was a transient temptation,
was at least an amusement.

I feel sad suddenly.
It's such a big, deep bowl,
like a reservoir drained of everything
but three little turtles.
I remember what my daughter said
as she practiced her long division:
Don't you kind of feel sorry for the remainders?

I should eat them, I know.
They haven't moved in days.
Winter is failing, but spring is weak, too,
Easter past, the ham bone bare.
Always there is some useless reminder
of better times, something absently picked up
and quietly laid back down.

Six Months After My Father's Death

It was Mother on the phone, and she sounded
well, finally out of his misery.

Her breathing was good, her lungs
clear, after the near suffocation

of his last year. He hadn't meant to hurt her.
Drowning people will do anything for air.

Do you still hear his whistle? I asked,
and she said, "Sometimes it

wakes me in the morning, yes."
It had hung, silver and serene, near his hand

and in her last dream.
Or was it the mockingbird she heard

that took up the summons he had mastered?
What with her nearly deaf and him so feeble

some last calls surely went unanswered
and some answers came faithfully

in response to nothing
more than a gray bird perched

at the top of a lemon tree,
pleading for help.

Honey

Luxury itself, thick as a Persian carpet,
honey fills the jar
with the concentrated sweetness
of countless thefts,
the blossoms bereft, the hive destitute.

Though my debts are heavy
honey would pay them all.
Honey heals, honey mends.
A spoon takes more than it can hold
without reproach. A knife plunges deep,
but does no injury.

Honey moves with intense deliberation.
Between one drop and the next
forty lean years pass in a distant desert.
What one generation labored for
another receives,
and yet another gives thanks.

Leftovers

After you have read all you possibly can
there may be a few lines left.
Please don't feel obligated!
They're cold by now
as conclusions often are.
Hard, too, like beef fat that
whitens at the foot of a roast.
Some can make another meal of leftovers
and often read past midnight
drinking the last wine
directly out of the bottle.
"Happily ever after" is for those
who never seem to tire of sweets.
And you: you're already going home,
leaving me with this mess,
wrinkled napkins, bones and crusts
and onions teased out of the salad.
If only I had a pig to fatten
on last words.

Ice Out

The south wind discovers a loose thread
and winter begins to unravel.
The first black and blue butterfly
materializes. The second.
They find each other.

The snow fort is in ruins.
Stacks of ammunition
have melted into the grass.
A floatplane with stiff wings
banks over the pines, turning north;
an eagle, too, searches for open water.

Open water. A window to the bottom.
Sometimes the water is so clear
that it hardly exists
except as a change in viscosity.
The island has its moat again,
the moon its mirror.

About the Author

Connie Wanek was born in 1952 in Madison, Wisconsin, and grew up in Las Cruces, New Mexico. In 1989 she moved with her family to Duluth, Minnesota, where she now lives. Her two previous books of poetry are *Bonfire* (New Rivers Press, 1997) and *Hartley Field* (Holy Cow! Press, 2002). She served as co-editor of a comprehensive, historical anthology of Minnesota women poets, called *To Sing Along the Way* (New Rivers Press, 2006). Ted Kooser, Poet Laureate of the United States (2004–2006), named her a Witter Bynner Fellow of the Library of Congress for 2006.

LANNAN LITERARY SELECTIONS

For two decades Lannan Foundation has supported the publication and distribution of exceptional literary works. Copper Canyon Press gratefully acknowledges their support.

LANNAN LITERARY SELECTIONS 2009

Michael Dickman, *The End of the West*
James Galvin, *As Is*
Heather McHugh, *Upgraded to Serious*
Lucia Perillo, *Inseminating the Elephant*
Connie Wanek, *On Speaking Terms*

RECENT LANNAN LITERARY SELECTIONS FROM COPPER CANYON PRESS

Lars Gustafsson, *A Time in Xanadu,* translated by John Irons

David Huerta, *Before Saying Any of the Great Words: Selected Poems,* translated by Mark Schafer

June Jordan, *Directed by Desire: The Collected Poems*

Sarah Lindsay, *Twigs and Knucklebones*

W.S. Merwin, *Migration: New & Selected Poems*

Valzhyna Mort, *Factory of Tears,* translated by Franz Wright and Elizabeth Oehlkers Wright

Taha Muhammad Ali, *So What: New & Selected Poems, 1971–2005,* translated by Peter Cole, Yahya Hijazi, and Gabriel Levin

Dennis O'Driscoll, *Reality Check*

Kenneth Rexroth, *The Complete Poems of Kenneth Rexroth*

Ruth Stone, *In the Next Galaxy*

C.D. Wright, *One Big Self: An Investigation*

Matthew Zapruder, *The Pajamaist*

For a complete list of Lannan Literary Selections from Copper Canyon Press, please visit Partners on our Web site:
www.coppercanyonpress.org

The Chinese character for poetry is made up of two parts: "word" and "temple." It also serves as pressmark for Copper Canyon Press.

Since 1972, Copper Canyon Press has fostered the work of emerging, established, and world-renowned poets for an expanding audience. The Press thrives with the generous patronage of readers, writers, booksellers, librarians, teachers, students, and funders—everyone who shares the belief that poetry is vital to language and living.

Major funding has been provided by:
Amazon.com
Anonymous
Beroz Ferrell & The Point, LLC
Golden Lasso
Lannan Foundation
National Endowment for the Arts
Cynthia Lovelace Sears and Frank Buxton
Washington State Arts Commission

For information and catalogs:
COPPER CANYON PRESS
Post Office Box 271
Port Townsend, Washington 98368
360-385-4925
www.coppercanyonpress.org

The poems have been typeset in Centaur, an old-style serif typeface originally drawn as titling capitals by Bruce Rogers in 1914 for the Metropolitan Museum of Art. Headings are set in Requiem, an old-style serif typeface designed by Jonathan Hoefler in 1992 for licensing by his own foundry, Hoefler & Frere-Jones. Book design and composition by Phil Kovacevich. Printed on archival-quality paper at McNaughton & Gunn, Inc.